CRYPTOCURRENCY

Mining, trading and investing in the most
famous and profitable cryptocurrencies:
Bitcoin, Ethereum, Litecoin, Dash, NEM,
Ripple, Monero, and Others

The author of this book has taken careful measures to share vital information about the subject. May its readers acquire the right knowledge, wisdom, inspiration, and succeed.

Table of Contents

INTRODUCTION

Congratulations on downloading this book and thank you for doing so.

The following chapters will teach you the ins and outs of investing in cryptocurrencies. *Now* is the time for you to learn how to take advantage of the cryptocurrency market and start earning continuous profits:

Chapter 1 lays down the basics, that will help you to have a better understanding of the cryptocurrency market. This is the foundation that you need before you start making an investment.

Chapter 2 talks about the different cryptocurrencies in the market, such as Bitcoin, Ethereum, Zcash, Ripple, OmiseGO, Dash, and others.

Chapter 3 discusses the different types of cryptocurrency wallets. Before you can start using cryptocurrencies, you first need to know the correct wallet type that will suit your needs.

Chapter 4 talks about the different ways to mine cryptocurrencies. This is another option that you have when you invest in cryptocurrencies.

Chapter 5 lays down the standards that you should look for in a cryptocurrency trading broker. It is important that you work with a reliable and trustworthy broker.

Chapter 6 discusses the powerful strategies that you can use to turn the odds in your favor and completely dominate the cryptocurrency market.

Chapter 7 reveals the professional trading practices that you should learn and observe to further increase your chances of making a profit.

May this book be your guiding light to success and financial freedom.

There are plenty of books on this subject on the market,

thanks again for choosing this one! Every effort was made to ensure it is full of as much useful information as possible. Please enjoy!

CHAPTER 1

CRYPTOCURRENCY 101

What is a cryptocurrency?

A cryptocurrency is a kind of digital asset. It is held electronically (online) and has no physical existence. It primarily functions as a substitute for money. It is secured using the technology known as *cryptography*. Cryptography refers to the practice of securing information by converting it into codes. It was extensively used during the Second World War. At that time, it was important for the military to ensure that their communication with one another was secured and protected against the enemy. This only goes to show how much you can trust and depend on this technology.

To date, there are more than 1,000 cryptocurrencies being traded in the market. However, only a few of them can attract the interest of the people and can gain significant value. Among all the cryptocurrencies being traded, the number one and most successful cryptocurrency is Bitcoin. As of January 11, 2018, the price of 1 bitcoin is around $14,520 USD.

Cryptocurrencies are not considered as fiat money. What is *fiat money*? Fiat money refers to the official currency of a state. A good example of fiat money is the US dollar. Since cryptocurrencies are not considered as fiat money, they are also not considered as legal tender. Legal tender refers to that which a debtor can compel his/her creditor to accept payment. Of course, the exception here is if payment in cryptocurrency is also stipulated in the contract. It is noteworthy that even though cryptocurrencies are not considered as fiat money and legal tender, there are still many individuals and merchants around the world who accept cryptocurrencies as a medium of payments, such as Overdrive, Microsoft, Steam, Virgin Galactic, Peach Airlines, and Tesla, among many others.

Cryptocurrency users also enjoy anonymity. In a cryptocurrency transaction, only the cryptocurrency wallet address and the amount involved are usually revealed. Other information as to the name, address, and other personal details of the parties involved remain confidential. Cryptocurrencies also have a decentralized network, which means that it is not controlled by any government. Hence, it is easy to understand why there are states that may impose strict regulations upon the use of cryptocurrencies in their jurisdiction. This is because cryptocurrencies may be used in criminal activities, such as in money laundering and tax evasion. It is noteworthy that cryptocurrencies are generally legal, especially in the United States, Canada, Europe, Singapore, Philippines, Korea, and many others. The use of cryptocurrencies is only considered illegal in a few states like Ecuador, Bolivia, Morocco, and Algeria, and few other states. Some time ago, Russia used to outlaw the use of cryptocurrencies in its territory. Today, cryptocurrencies are now legal in Russia. Singapore also declared that it would not issue any restriction on the use of cryptocurrencies in its territory. Although China closed down its local crypto-currency exchanges, it was for the purpose of preparing certain restrictions or form of control, but this does not mean that it would no longer participate in the cryptocurrency market. More and more states and businesses are being open to the idea of using cryptocurrencies. Experts predict that there will soon come a time when cryptocurrencies will be the usual medium of exchange that will be used, especially that we live in a modern era of computers and the Internet.

Blockchain technology

The blockchain technology, or simply *blockchain*, is the backbone technology of bitcoin and other cryptocurrencies. It is defined as a decentralized and public distributed ledger that has a high security. It functions as a repository of cryptocurrency transactions and records. It is public in the sense that all the records on the blockchain are viewable and verifiable by everyone on the network. This gives it a sense of complete transparency. It is also decentralized because there is no central organization or government that has control over it. This ensures fairness and that it is free from any and all forms of undue influence and manipulation. The blockchain technology is composed of records known as *blocks*. Every new block is connected to the block that comes before it using a hash pointer. Hence, all the blocks are interconnected with one another. No block can be changed or altered without altering or affecting all the other blocks on the chain. Also, every update on the blockchain such as when a new block is added will also reflect on all the ledgers as shown to all the users. This is the concept of the distributed ledger. The blockchain technology also has a high security. For an attack against the blockchain to be successful, it has to possess at least 51% of the total hash rate of the entire blockchain. Since the blockchain is spread over a vast network of computers, it is virtually impossible for a hacker to meet the 51% requirement. This makes blockchain virtually invulnerable to attacks. Hence, it is trusted by countless of people worldwide.

The blockchain technology can still be considered a new technology. There is still so much that can be expected from it in the future. It is also noteworthy that this technology is making a name for itself aside from being closely associated with bitcoin and other cryptocurrencies. It has been found that this technology can be used for purposes other than recording cryptocurrency transactions and beyond the use of financial sectors. Indeed, this technology is something that you should keep an eye on. In fact, even those who are not in favor of the use of cryptocurrencies appreciate and find value in blockchain technology.

Why trade/invest in cryptocurrencies?

It is true that although cryptocurrencies function as a substitute for money, many of those who possess cryptocurrencies do not use them as such. Instead, they consider cryptocurrencies as a lucrative form of investment. There are people in the world who have earned millions just by investing in cryptocurrencies. Here is a classic example: If you had invested even just a small amount of $400 in bitcoins in 2009 or even in 2010, then you would have been a multimillionaire by now. Investing in cryptocurrencies can be highly profitable, especially if you understand the ins and outs of the market. Instead of investing in stocks where an annual profit of 50% is already considered very high, you can earn even more than 500% in just a few days or weeks when you invest in cryptocurrencies. Needless to say, bitcoin is not the only lucrative cryptocurrency in the market. In 2017, the altcoin, OmiseGO, which is just considered a minor cryptocurrency, increased by more than 1,200% in just a few weeks. There are various examples of highly profitable price fluctuations in the cryptocurrency market. Even today, these kinds of profits are considered normal, which is why so many people are eager to learn how to participate in the cryptocurrency market. There are many real-life success stories of people who have earned millions and even paved their way to financial freedom because of their investment in cryptocurrency. This is the best thing about investing in cryptocurrency: You can earn as little and as high as you can. If you stick to the lessons in this book, and you will be able to unveil the secrets on how you can turn the cryptocurrency market into a goldmine of high profits.

Just like any other kind of investment, there are also risks involved when you invest in cryptocurrency. Although you can earn a high amount of profit, there is also the possibility that you may lose your investment. However, if you do your research and take necessary effort to understand the market, then you can significantly increase your chance of making a profit and minimize your risks. There are many professional cryptocurrency investors/traders who have quit their day job and trade/invest in cryptocurrencies as a full-time profession. Of course, there are also those who have profited a very high amount that they no longer need to work even for a day. The point here is that this kind of success story is possible, and you can make this happen in your life by learning how to trade and/or invest in the cryptocurrency market.

Trading vs. Buying

The terms *trading* and *buying* are often used synonymously. However, for the word geeks out there, there are certain differences between the two. On the one hand, when you *buy* cryptocurrencies, it involves actually buying cryptocurrencies. To make a profit, then you need to engage in a buy and sell activity, which is merely about buying low and selling high via an exchange platform. When you do this, you offer your cryptocurrencies at full value when you open a position. On the other hand, when you *trade* cryptocurrencies, you make a speculation when a particular market will rise or fall. Take note that unlike buying cryptocurrencies, you do not take ownership of the cryptocurrencies that you trade, but you merely speculate as to their price movements. Trading also usually involves what is known as margin trading. Margin trading is like the forex where you can leverage your position by borrowing cryptocurrencies from your trading broker. This way you can trade with much bigger funds even if you do not really have a well-funded trading account. Needless to say, this will allow you to earn a really high amount of profit even if you only invested a small capital. However, this approach is not advisable for beginners as it can be costly in the long run since you will have to pay interest to your trading broker.

Understanding high volatility

The cryptocurrency market is known for having high volatility. But, what does *high volatility* really mean?

When you say that the cryptocurrency market has a high volatility, it means that the price of the cryptocurrencies fluctuates rapidly and significantly. To give you an example, there was a time when the price of bitcoin increase by $2,000 in just a few days, but there was also an incident when its price dropped also by $2,000 just as fast. It should also be noted that high volatility is not something that balances itself out in the long run. A common misconception of high volatility is that after a significant increase in price, then it would be followed by a significant decrease in price, and vice versa. However, this is not always the case. It is possible for an increase in price to be followed by another increase or even a series of increases. In the same way, a drop in price and still be followed by another significant decrease or even a series of decreases. Of course, the rise and fall of the price of a cryptocurrency can also happen in a seemingly random manner. The point here is that the cryptocurrency market does not balance itself out unless there are factors that will move the price of a cryptocurrency to do so. This means that cryptocurrencies do not move at random but are influenced by numerous factors and elements, such as the economy, the competition among the different cryptocurrencies, market acceptance, the news, and other technological developments, among other things.

CHAPTER 2

BITCOIN & ALTCOINS

It is a common knowledge that the number one crypto-currency in the world is Bitcoin. In fact, it is considered as the leading standard that all other cryptocurrencies are merely referred to as altcoins, which is short for *alternative coins*. Still, it is worth noting that trading and investing in altcoins can also be highly lucrative. Therefore, as a cryptocurrency investor, it is also important for you to be aware of the different altcoins in the market. Let us look at some of the known and less-known cryptocurrencies:

✓ Bitcoin

When it comes to cryptocurrencies, Bitcoin always tops

the list. It cannot be denied that bitcoin is the most popular, successful, and highly priced cryptocurrency in the world. As of January 11, 2018, the price of 1 bitcoin is around $14,520 USD. In 2008, a paper was posted on a cryptography mailing list by Satoshi Nakamoto. The title was *Bitcoin: A Peer-to-Peer Electronic Cash System*. In 2009, Bitcoin was finally launched in the market. Back then, bitcoin did not have any significant value. It was the cryptocurrency community itself who decided how much they wanted it to be worth. In fact, there was this transaction where two pizzas delivered by Papa John's were purchased for 10,000 bitcoins. The offer was made on the bitcointalk forum. Up to now, you can view the thread on the said forum, and you will see how many people at that time did not realize just how valuable bitcoin would be. Bitcoin is also the first decentralized network that runs on blockchain technology. Another interesting fact about bitcoin is that although it is the most successful cryptocurrency, the identity of its creator, Satoshi Nakamoto, remains a mystery. The name Satoshi Nakamoto is just a pseudonym. Nakamoto has also withdrawn from the public for years. There are many theories regarding Nakamoto's true identity: Some say that Satoshi Nakamoto is composed of a group of computer experts. Others say that Nakamoto is Hal Finney, the first man who downloaded the bitcoin software and received 10 bitcoins from Satoshi Nakamoto just for downloading the software; however, Hal Finney denied this claim. There are also others who even claim that Satoshi Nakamoto is a woman. Still, there is no one who could guarantee with 100% certainty the true identity of Satoshi Nakamoto. Even though the creator of bitcoin remains a mystery, the fruit of his labor remains the number one and most popular cryptocurrency in the world.

✓ Ethereum

Ethereum is considered as the second most successful cryptocurrency next to bitcoin. It should be noted that Ethereum is the platform, and its token is called ether. As of January 11, 2008, the price of 1 ether is around 1,216 USD. It was introduced in the market in 2015. Ether is not just any other kind of cryptocurrency. The Ethereum platform allows the use of smart contracts and distributed applications on its blockchain. According to

Ethereum, it can "codify, decentralize, secure and trade just about anything." Smart Contracts execute contracts provided certain conditions are met. Although a smart contract can only execute simple tasks, you can use many smart contracts for more complicated tasks. Since the Ethereum platform allows the use of smart contracts and distributed applications, it has also become the technology that is used by other altcoins. Many people believe that Ethereum will soon take the place of bitcoin as the number one cryptocurrency in the world. However, if you look at the past and present trend, this seems to be far from happening. Still, it cannot be denied that Ethereum is one of the most profitable and successful cryptocurrencies in the market today.

✓ Litecoin

Litecoin is not a new player in the market. It was launched in 2011 by an ex-Google engineer and MIT graduate, Charles Lee. It was one of the early competitors of bitcoin. Litecoin functions just like bitcoin and is also based on an open and decentralized source. Its aim is to be the better version of bitcoin. It can generate blocks faster than bitcoin. This means that it can confirm and complete transactions faster. Many merchants also accept payments in Litecoin. As of January 11, 2018, the price of 1 Litecoin is around $230 USD.

✓ Dash

Dash quickly gained its own following after its launch in 2014. Back then, it was called as Darkcoin. Although the name changed into Dash or Dash coin, which is short for Digital Cash, its features remain the same. Dash offers a higher level of anonymity and privacy. As of January 11, 2018, the price of 1 Dash coin is around $1,059 USD.

✓ NEM

NEM was introduced in the market in 2015. It is also a peer-to-peer network. It is written in Java. Its aim is to have a wide distribution model. It also has interesting features on its blockchain, such as using multi-sig accounts, POI algorithm, and encrypted messaging, among others. Its developers remain unknown, but it was started by a user in the Bitcoin talk forum known as UtopianFuture. As of the start of 2018, it is not doing well in the market. Its price as of January 11, 2018, is just around $1.35 after a price decrease of around 8%.

✓ Ripple

A key distinction between Ripple and other cryptocurrencies is that it does not take the place of banks. Instead, it supports and helps banks in their transactions. Ripple "enables banks to settle cross-border payments in real time, with end-to-end transparency, and at lower costs." Ripple has been gaining lots of attention and interest as of the beginning of 2018. It was even tagged as the second largest cryptocurrency in terms of market capitalization. As of January 11, 2018, the price of 1 Ripple is around $1.71 USD.

✓ Monero

Monero is a community-driven cryptocurrency. It relied on mere donations from the cryptocurrency community. It was introduced in the market in 2014. This cryptocurrency allows transactions to have complete privacy by using *ring signatures*. When you use ring signatures, a legitimate transaction is combined together with false transactions. Hence, when you view the transactions on the blockchain, it would be hard, if not impossible, to identify which transaction is legitimate and valid from those that are false. Monero focuses on scalability and decentralization. As of January 11, 2018, the price of 1 Monero is around $371 USD.

✓ Lisk

Lisk is a new player in the cryptocurrency market. It was introduced in 2016, and it allows its users to use what is called as Software Development Kit (SDK). This allows its users to deploy their very own blockchain and even use decentralized applications on it. Hence, Lisk allows you to create games, platforms, messengers, and other exciting apps, by allowing you to build your own block-chain on top of the original Lisk blockchain. Lisk also focuses on decentralization. As of January 11, 2018, its price is around $26.

✓ Zcash

Zcash is a favorite among those who place high value on one's privacy and anonymity. Zcash allows its users to hide not only the name of the recipient and the sender but also the amount that is involved in a transaction. It places importance on privacy and security. Zcash rightly describes itself that "If Bitcoin is like http for money, Zcash is https." As of January 11, 2018, the price of 1 Zcash (ZEC) is around $647 USD.

✓ IOTA

IOTA claims to be the cryptocurrency that is specially designed for the Internet of Things. It uses a technology known a *Tangle*. Unlike Bitcoin and other cryptocurrencies that uses a blockchain system to update their ledger, IOTA uses Tangle to solve the transaction fees and scalability normally encountered in bitcoin and other altcoins based on blockchain technology. This is done by requiring the sender to do some sort of proof of work to approve two transactions. This refers to both the act of making and validating a transaction. As a result, the system for transferring funds become completely decentralized as there is no need for miners to verify a transaction. Another interesting development of IOTA is that the more users are on its network, the speed of its network transaction also increases. Simply put, this is the way to making completely zero-cost transactions. As of January 11, 2018, the price of 1 IOTA is around $3.33 USD.

✓ OmiseGO

Back in 2017, the price of this cryptocurrency increased by more than 1,000% in a span of a few weeks. It has an ambitious aim to "unbank the banked using cryptocurrency technology." It is also one of those altcoins that are based on the Ethereum platform. Although its dramatic increase in price in 2017 became very famous, many believe that it was due to a mere pump and dump scheme. AS of January 11, 2018, the price of this cryptocurrency is around $20 after a drop in price of around 15%.

There are many other altcoins in the market, and many are still expected to come. As you can notice, due to the tight competition, cryptocurrencies make sure that they offer value to the market. The people have to see that a certain cryptocurrency is something valuable; otherwise, it will most likely end up being ignored just like other cryptocurrencies. With more and more cryptocurrencies to choose from, there are also more opportunities for you to make a profit.

CHAPTER 3

CRYPTOCURRENCY WALLETS

Why do you need a cryptocurrency wallet?

Before you can start using and investing in cryptocurrencies, you first need to have a place where you can store them. This place where you store your cryptocurrencies is referred to as a *cryptocurrency wallet*. There are many wallet providers out there, but you need to use the right wallet type that will best suit your needs. Generally, cryptocurrency wallets are divided into two main kinds: hot and cold wallet. A hot wallet is a cryptocurrency wallet that exists online. Hence, it is very convenient to use. It is also the most common type of cryptocurrency wallet. Good examples of hot wallets are Coinbase and Exodus. The problem with using a hot wallet is that it offers less security. For example, if a hacker manages to hack into Coinbase and you have a hot wallet account with Coinbase, then there is a chance that you may no longer recover your stolen cryptocurrencies. Still, many cryptocurrency users use hot wallets. A cold wallet is also known as cold storage. This is the kind of wallet that is stored offline. Hence, it is not exposed to the risks and hazards of the Internet, which makes it very secure. Good examples of cold wallets are Trezor and KeepKey. Now, hot and cold wallets are further divided into different types:

The different types of cryptocurrency wallets

✓ Web wallet

This is the most commonly used type of cryptocurrency wallet. It is also called as Internet wallet or online wallet. This is the kind of wallet where you store your private and public keys online. The first step is to sign up for an account with a hot wallet provider like Coinbase. You can always access and manage your wallet simply by accessing it on the Internet. Hence, a web wallet is very convenient to use. It should be noted that many web wallets have already updated their security features. Still, if you want to use a wallet that has the best security, then you should opt for a cold wallet.

✓ Mobile wallet

A mobile wallet is another type of hot wallet. As the name already suggests, a mobile wallet is the type of wallet that you can download on your mobile device. Usually, you will be able to download the application from the Apple or GooglePlay store for free. You can then access and manage your cryptocurrencies from your mobile phone. Wallet providers are aware that people these days normally access the Internet using their mobile device. Hence, a mobile version of the wallet is also provided. Most web wallets also offer a mobile wallet version.

✓ Software wallet

A software wallet is a type of hot wallet. You can download a software wallet on your computer. You then have to use your computer to access your wallet. Although this may seem like a cold wallet, it is still considered a hot wallet because the computer can still be connected to the Internet and be used for surfing websites. Therefore, it can still be a target for hackers and be prone to viruses and malware.

✓ Desktop wallet

A desktop wallet is a kind of cols wallet. When you use a desktop wallet, you store your private and private keys in a computer. It is noteworthy that although this wallet is referred to as a "desktop" wallet, the computer that you use does not necessarily have to be a desktop computer. Hence, it can just be a laptop computer. It is important for you to ensure that the computer is functioning properly as it would be hard to recover your public and private keys if your computer suddenly malfunctions. Before you use anything as a desktop wallet, it is strongly advised that you reformat the computer prior to using it as a wallet. This is to remove any virus or malware that may have attached itself to your computer. High security is the main feature of a cold wallet, so keep it your number one priority. Needless to say, you should avoid connecting the computer that you are using as a desktop wallet to the Internet.

✓ Hardware wallet

A hardware wallet is another kind of cold wallet. Just like a desktop wallet, you will have to store your private and public keys offline. However, instead of storing them in a computer, you get to store them in some form of hardware like a USB. There is also a specialized kind of hardware these days that are made for the sole purpose of being used as a cold wallet. It will have a button that you need to press before you can send any of your cryptocurrencies. This ensures that before your cryptocurrencies can be moved or transferred to another, the person must have the hardware wallet in his/her possession. To date, there is no record or report that a hardware wallet has been successfully hacked. Just take note that although a cold wallet can protect you from the hazards of the Internet, it does not protect you from physical risks like getting your cold wallet stolen, lost, or broken. Therefore, always exercise caution and diligence.

✓ Paper wallet

A paper wallet is another popular kind of cryptocurrency cold wallet. When you use a paper wallet, you can print your public and private keys on a paper. It is suggested that you keep several copies for yourself just in case you lose the original copy. Of course, you will have to hide them in a secure and safe place where other people would not be able to find them. Many paper wallets these days can also provide you with a QR code that you can scan before you can access your cryptocurrencies.

So, which wallet type is for you?

The right type of wallet for you would depend on how you intend to use cryptocurrencies. If you intend to send cryptocurrencies on a regular basis, then a hot wallet will most probably be the better choice. If you intend to hold on to a particular cryptocurrency for a long-term, for example, when making a long-term investment, then you may want to use a cold wallet. Keep in mind that you are not limited to using just a single type of wallet. There are many cryptocurrency traders out there who use both cold and hot wallets at the same time, depending on how they intend to use their cryptocurrencies. You are also free to use multiple hot wallets if you want. Again, how you intend to use cryptocurrencies is the main factor that you should consider when deciding on the right and suitable wallet type for you.

CHAPTER 4

CRYPTOCURRENCY MINING

What is the importance of mining?

Before a new block is added to the blockchain, the block, record, or transaction, must first be confirmed and verified. This process of confirmation and verification is done through mining. Hence, there is always a demand for miners for blockchain-based cryptocurrencies like bitcoin. Miners receive a reward every time they solve and mine a new block in the form of transaction fee. Without miners, no new record or block will be added to the blockchain which means that no transaction can be made. There are different ways to mine for cryptocurrencies. Let us look at them one by one:

The different ways to mine cryptocurrencies

➢ Computer mining

You can mine using your computer. For example, you can download GUIMiner, join a mining pool, and start mining bitcoins using your computer. However, a computer alone does not have enough hash power to mine a decent amount of cryptocurrency. You will probably end up paying more for your electric expenses than the amount of cryptocurrency that you could mine. But, if you just want to experience how it feels like to mine cryptocurrencies on your own and do not mind earning a very small amount, then computer mining is a good start. When you use your computer to mine, be careful with overheating. Do not mine for long hours as your computer can overheat and even be broken. Follow a schedule and make sure to give time for your computer to cool down. If you are serious about making a decent profit, then you should consider getting a hardware, and this leads us to the next type of mining known as hardware mining.

➢ Hardware mining

Since a computer alone does not have enough mining power to earn you a decent amount of cryptocurrency, you may want to do hardware mining. When you use hardware mining, you will mine using both your computer and a mining hardware. This way you will have more mining power that will enable you to mine more cryptocurrencies. Again, be careful with overheating issues. Be sure to follow a schedule and allow your computer and hardware to cool down. A drawback of using hardware mining is that a high-quality mining hardware can be expensive. It will take some time before you can recover your investment in buying a hardware.

➢ Software mining

With this mining method, you will download a software on your computer and use it to mine for cryptocurrencies. Normally, you will have to purchase it from a company. The software provider may also allow you to upgrade your account to mine for more cryptocurrencies. Of course, an additional fee is often imposed for upgrading your account or software. Again, since you will still be using your computer, you will have to pay attention to any overheating problems, and you still need to mine cryptocurrencies yourself.

➤ Cloud mining

Cloud mining is the most popular type of method for mining nowadays. With cloud mining, you no longer have to use your computer nor worry about any overheating issue. Instead, you simply have to wait for a mining company to send you cryptocurrencies, which is normally on a weekly/monthly basis, or every time that you reach the minimum threshold amount.

Of course, no mining company will send you cryptocurrencies just out of kindness. The catch here is that you first need to make an investment by paying the mining company. Here is how an offer may look like: Invest 0.5 bitcoins and receive up to 0.008 bitcoins every week. Although this may seem like a good enough deal, the problem is that what the mining company shows you is probably just the *expected* return and not the *actual* amount that you will receive. Before you deposit or invest any money, make sure to read the terms and conditions properly. You should also check the reviews given to the cloud mining company. Simply use your favorite browser and key in the name of the cloud mining company followed by the word "reviews." For example, if you want to know the reviews on the mining company known as Genesis Mining, just search for *Genesis Mining reviews*. The search engine results pages (SERP) will then provide you with related pages. Read the reviews and compare them with the reviews given to other cloud mining companies.

Note: Although it can still be profitable to earn a decent amount of profit by mining cryptocurrencies, many experts advise that if you want to earn a really high amount of profit, then you should learn to trade and/or invest in cryptocurrencies instead. The problem with mining is that the potential profit is usually limited, and there are also many problems that can occur, such as overheating, the expenses for buying a hardware or software, and others. Not to mention, there are also many scammers out there who simply want to rip you off of your money. But, if you really want to mine for cryptocurrencies, then this option can still be profitable.

CHAPTER 5

CRYPTOCURRENCY TRADING BROKER

As a cryptocurrency investor/trader, it is important that you work with a reliable and trustworthy trading broker. If you do a search online, you will easily find so many brokers that seem to offer you the same service. But, how do you know which of these brokers will best suit your needs? Here are the standards to look for:

✓ Trading platform

Your broker is the one that will provide you with the platform that you can use to buy and sell, as well as open trading positions. Hence, your broker should provide you with a professional-looking platform. Although the design of the platform may not be as important as its features, it is still beneficial to have a professionally designed platform as to help set the right mood for trading/investing. Your broker should also provide you with tools such as graphs that can help you come up with a sound trading decision. Simply put, the trading platform should make the experience of trading cryptocurrencies easy and convenient for you. You should also check the different cryptocurrencies traded by your broker. Of course, the more cryptocurrencies are available for trading, the more choices that you will have.

✓ Customer support

It is important that you work with a broker that has an active and professional customer support team. The customer support can help you in case you have questions and especially if you are having technical issues. Your broker will provide you with ways on how you can get in touch with the customer support team. Normally, an email address would be provided or a certain page on the platform may be used where you can directly send a message to the support team. A live on-page chat service may also be provided by your broker. Sometimes a broker may even provide you with a number that you can call to reach the customer support team.

It is suggested that you test the customer support to see how responsive it is. A good way of doing this is by testing the support team. Just send an inquiry and pay attention to how fast and professional it responds. You should be able to get a response within 24 hours. In your life as a cryptocurrency investor/trader, it is important for you to work only with a trading broker that has an active and professional customer support team.

✓ Latest reviews

Just like when looking for other services or products online, you should also read the latest reviews given to the trading broker that you intend to use. Be sure to read the reviews before you make any form of deposit. Also, do not rely on just one website for reviews. This is because many cryptocurrency trading brokers hire writers to come up with a positive write-up about their business. Hence, read as many reviews as you can. It is also good if you can read some negative reviews. This usually shows that the reviews are honest and true. To find the reviews on a particular broker, simply open your browser, type the name of the broker, and add the word "reviews." The SERP will then give you a list of related pages. Also, pay attention to the dates when the reviews were written.

✓ Mobile version

These days, it is much faster and convenient to access the Internet through your mobile phone. Trading brokers are well aware of this, and so many of them provide a mobile feature or version of the trading platform. All legitimate and high-quality cryptocurrency trading brokers offer a mobile version of their trading platform, so this is something that you should not worry about.

The mobile version should be easy and convenient to use. Although it may not provide all the features that you can enjoy when you use a desktop computer, it should at least provide you with the important parts of the trading platform. You should be able to manage your account easily, as well as open and close trading positions. It should also allow you to make deposits and withdrawals easily. Last but not least, it should be easy to use and navigate. Again, your trading broker should help you and make the experience of trading more convenient and interesting.

✓ Deposit and withdrawal limits and requirements

Check the minimum and maximum deposit and withdrawal requirements of your broker. Also, keep in mind that making a deposit is usually easier than making a withdrawal. Normally, making a deposit can be made instantly provided you transfer funds from your wallet into your trading account. However, when making a withdrawal, most brokers will require you to first submit some documents, such as a valid ID and a proof of billing, before it would process your withdrawal request. This is where the problem actually starts. Some people fail to make a successful withdrawal. Therefore, before you deposit anything into your trading account, be sure to be clear with your broker regarding its requirements for making a successful withdrawal; otherwise, you may risk having your funds and profits locked in your account without any way of withdrawing them. Be sure that you have the required documents in your possession, and make sure that they are still valid and have not yet expired. If you have questions or more concerns on this matter, do not hesitate to contact the customer support team.

Additional notes:

It is fast and easy to sign up for a trading account with a cryptocurrency trading broker. The process usually takes just around two minutes. The important thing is identifying which broker that you will use. Be careful because there are scammers out there who are always looking for their next victim. Hence, make sure that you work only with a reliable and trustworthy cryptocurrency trading broker.

Now, if you just want to purchase bitcoin or any other known cryptocurrencies and make a long-term investment, it should be noted that you may no longer need to use a trading broker. There are now many cryptocurrency wallets like Coinbase that will allow you to purchase cryptocurrencies directly from your cryptocurrency wallet account.

It bears stressing that you should not rush the process of choosing a cryptocurrency trading broker. It is very important that you get to work only with a trustworthy and reliable broker, so take as much time as you need to identify the right broker for you.

CHAPTER 6

POWERFUL AND EFFECTIVE STRATEGIES

✓ Fundamental analysis

Fundamental analysis is also called as the lifeblood of investment. The key to using this strategy is to gather as many information and real facts as possible. It stands on the premise that the more you understand a particular cryptocurrency, the more likely that you will be able to predict its price movement in the market. Hence, when you use fundamental analysis, you should follow the latest news. The news has a powerful influence on the price of a cryptocurrency. Just to give you an idea: When CNN featured just how high the price of bitcoin was increasing at that time, it further pushed the price of bitcoin even higher. When China declared that it would close down all its cryptocurrency exchanges, the price of bitcoin and other cryptocurrencies dropped. When Russia removed its ban on the use of bitcoins and other cryptocurrencies, the price of bitcoin experienced a significant increase in value. As you can see, by being aware of the latest news and analyzing its implications in the market, you can get a good idea of how the price of certain cryptocurrencies will most likely be affected.

The news is not the only source of information. You should also check the white paper released by the developer of a cryptocurrency. Although it may be hard to understand due to the technical terms, it will nonetheless provide you with useful information regarding the cryptocurrency. You should also join related online groups and forums. Many developers are active in these places, and this will allow you not only to get information from the developers, but you can even contact them if you want. Needless to say, you can also learn from the other members of the cryptocurrency community. From time to time, you will surely be able to read interesting points of view, as well as useful strategies that you can use to make a profit in the cryptocurrency market.

This strategy is important because it deals with the basics. If you do not understand the basics, then how do you think could you make the right investment decision? Therefore, always do your research and analysis of the different cryptocurrencies in the market. Do not be lazy.

Fundamental analysis can be used with other strategies. People usually use this strategy together with technical analysis. If you consider yourself as a true and professional cryptocurrency investor/trader, then it is a must that you observe this strategy regardless of other strategies that you may want to use. After all, if you do not know the fundamentals, it would be hard to think of yourself as a real investor/trader.

✓ Technical analysis

This is a favorite strategy among many cryptocurrency traders. When you use technical analysis, you will be dealing with graphs and charts that show the price movements of a particular cryptocurrency. Hence, if you are more of a visual person, then this is something that you should learn. Normally, your cryptocurrency trading broker will be the one that will provide you with free tools (charts and graphs) to use technical analysis. However, if such tools are not provided, you will definitely find many websites online that will give you the right tools for using technical analysis.

When you use this approach, you should learn to identify patterns. Okay, you might be wondering: *Do patterns really occur?* The answer is yes. In fact, even a completely random generator would generate patterns every now and then. To make a nice profit, you need to learn to spot patterns and take advantage of them. Beware of forcing a pattern. Some people think that they can see a pattern every time they examine a graph. This is wrong. Patterns come and go; therefore, just because you have been staring at the same graph for hours does not mean that you can always come up with a good investing decision.

The concept of this strategy is that all the factors that can affect the price of a cryptocurrency have their effect on the price. Therefore, by simply analyzing the price movements, you get to deal with all these factors. This saves you from the hassle of having to read and analyze tons of information. In a way, this is the opposite of financial analysis. However, it should be noted that if you are serious about making a profit, then you should not rely on patterns or trends alone. To further increase your chances of making the right and profitable decision, then you should apply technical analysis with another strategy. Normally, people use technical analysis with fundamental analysis. Many experts agree that mastery of both strategies and using them at the same time can increase your rate of success by more than 75%.

✓ Buy and hold

The buy and hold strategy is probably the simplest strategy that you can use. But, do not underestimate this strategy. Indeed, there are people who have earned millions and even financial freedom simply by relying on this strategy. AS the name implies, this is about buying cryptocurrencies, and then holding on to it for some time to allow its price to increase. You can then sell them at a profit. Remember the classic example: Had you invested even just $400 in bitcoins back in 2009 or 2010, then you would have earned millions by now. Needless to say, this strategy applies even to altcoins. However, do not use this strategy blindly. You cannot just buy and hold any cryptocurrency at random. To increase your chances of success, the first thing that you should do is to study the cryptocurrency that you intend to invest in. Analyze it to find out if it is a profitable investment or not. If there are good reasons to believe that it is a profitable investment, then that is the time for you to apply this strategy.

✓ Altcoin spread out

To date, there are more than 1,000 altcoins that have already been created. Some of these altcoins can establish themselves in the market like Ethereum, Zcash, and others. It is not a secret that bitcoin is not the only cryptocurrency that can be considered profitable. In fact, there are many altcoins in the market even today that increase by more than 500% in value within a short span of time. Hence, investing in the right altcoins can also be highly profitable. In fact, due to the high price of bitcoin, many people these days prefer to invest in altcoins.

The proper way to use this strategy is to divide your capital. There is no hard and fast rule as to how many times you should divide your capital, but it is suggested that you divide it to at least five. Hence, if you have an invested capital worth $1,000, you should be able to invest in five positions in the amount of $200 per position. Hence, if you have 1 bitcoin, you will have at least five positions with 0.2 bitcoin per position. Take note that five is only the suggested *minimum* number of times to divide your capital; you can divide your capital into 10 or even 20 if you want. Now, the key is to identify valuable and profitable altcoins to invest in. Therefore, you should study the different altcoins in the market, preferably the new and start-up altcoins as such altcoins have a big room for growth. Just imagine the more than 1,000% increase in price experienced by the altcoin, OmiseGO, in a few weeks back in 2017. If you hit this kind of investment, then you would still end up in a positive profit even if you lose some of your other investments. This is actually the objective of this strategy: To identify and invest in highly profitable altcoins.

A common mistake is to get careless and take some of

your investments for granted. Some people tend to be lazy and careless because they are aware that they are going to make multiple positions anyway. Hence, they can afford to lose out some trades or investments. This is wrong. Keep in mind that every investment or trade that you make should be backed up by heavy research and analysis. If you are not confident of a particular position, then do not make any investment. Never take any trade or investment for granted. Also, every new position that you open is distinct and different from your previous positions or trades. Again, be careful and never take any position for granted. It is better for you to be inactive and not make any investment at all than to invest in something that you have researched and analyzed properly.

✓ Averaging down

This is an excellent strategy that will allow you to purchase a cryptocurrency at a "bargain" and be able to sell it at a high profit. The best way to explain this strategy is through an example: Let us say that you want to invest in bitcoin. Let us assume that the current price of bitcoin is $12,000. You should make a buy order at the said price of $12,000. Now, if the price of bitcoin increases, then you can sell at a profit. However, if the price decreases, you should make another buy order. Hence, if the price drops, say, down to $11,500, then you should make a buy order at the said lower amount of $11,500. Now, let us assume that the price continues to decrease, say, down to $11,000, then you should make another buy order at the said lower amount of $11,000. You should continue to follow the same buying pattern as much as you like. Okay, so you must be thinking: Are you not simply investing in a losing asset? The answer is *no*. In fact, you are making a profitable investment. The key to profit is when the price either recovers back to its original value (price of the cryptocurrency when you first applied the strategy), or higher. When this happens, all the buy orders that you have made will experience a nice profit. This is why it is important that before you use this strategy, you should first study the market and identify the cryptocurrency that will most likely be profitable.

It should be noted that this strategy is considered highly aggressive. When using any aggressive strategy, it is recommended that you limit your risk by using a stop-loss limit. How do you use a stop-loss limit? You should set a limitation prior to making any investment. For example, if you use averaging down and set a stop-loss limit of 4. This means that you will only make up to 4 buy orders. If the price continues to drop after the said 4 buy orders, then you will no longer continue to chase it down. This way you can minimize your exposure. After all, the cryptocurrency market can be highly volatile. Remember an excellent example in the past when the price of bitcoin dropped by around $2,000 very quickly. Although the averaging down strategy appears to be a highly effective and powerful strategy, it is still considered an aggressive strategy, so be careful every time that you use it.

✓ Cryptocoin mastery

It is true that the more that you know and understand a particular cryptocurrency the more likely that you can predict its price movement in the market. This is exactly the key to using this strategy. When you use cryptocoin mastery, you should choose a single cryptocurrency in the market that you think would be profitable. It is suggested that you focus on altcoins, especially the new ones. Now, your job is to study the said altcoin on a daily basis. Your objective is to gain mastery over it. You will know if you already have a good level of mastery once you can predict its price movements correctly with at least 80% success rate. Once you achieve this level, then that is the only time for you to make an investment. This strategy might take weeks or even months for you to complete since you still need to gain mastery over a particular cryptocurrency. Do not rush the learning process as it is the key that will allow you to make a profit. Now, it can also happen that while you are studying a particular cryptocurrency, you may suddenly realize that it is not a profitable investment at all. When this happens, simply switch to another cryptocurrency. Do not worry; this is normal. The life of a cryptocurrency investor is full of trials and errors, but it is through this process that you learn and grow as professional cryptocurrency investor/trader.

✓ Pump and dump advantage

Before discussing how to use this strategy, you need to understand how the famous pump and dump scheme works. This is not a new scheme. In fact, it is used by some groups in the stock market. So, how does it work? As the name already suggests, it is where a certain cryptocurrency is pumped. This is where an individual or a group attempts to make the price of a particular cryptocurrency that they have to increase through the use of promotions. The problem with this is that it is usually done through the use of false promotions where you make a bad investment to appear as if it were profitable. This is why it is not a recommended method since it is fraudulent. Now, due to the promotional hype, it will draw the interest of some people which would lead them to make an investment in the cryptocurrency that is made the subject of the said scheme. Of course, this will further increase the price of the cryptocurrency that is being pumped, which will make it look even more convincing, especially if it gets featured on the news. Once the people behind the scheme are happy with the increase in value that they have made, they can now sell the said cryptocurrency. This is the part where the people responsible for the scheme now dump the cryptocurrency. The effect of this is that the people behind the pump and dump scheme will enjoy a nice profit while all the other investors will realize that they have become victims and would be holding a losing asset whose price simply keeps on decreasing. The problem with this scheme is that there is no real value. This is why you should check if the price of a cryptocurrency is really as its value deserves.

Now that you know how a pump and dump works, it is time for you to learn how to take advantage of it. Take note that this book does not encourage anyone to participate in a pump and dump scheme due to its fraudulent nature. Instead, this book teaches how you can turn such fraud into profit without directly participating in the fraud. As you can see, in a pump and dump scheme, the price of the cryptocurrency involved really increases. This is your key to profit. It is only when the cryptocurrency gets dumped when the investors will suffer a loss; however, before the cryptocurrency gets dumped, everyone is happy with their investment. Hence, the key is to identify a pump and dump when it is taking place. You should then make an investment in the cryptocurrency that is being promoted while the scheme is still in the beginning stage, and then the most important part is to exit your position way before the cryptocurrency gets dumped. A usual sign of a pump and dump scheme is the increasing price of a cryptocurrency without a real basis other than the fact that it is being promoted. This is another reason why fundamental analysis is very important as it allows you to understand the market much better than any other strategy. Again, when you ride on a pump and dump scheme, it is important that you should not be greedy. Remember that you cannot control the group behind it, so you would not know exactly when it is going to dump the cryptocurrency that is subject to the scheme. Hence, the best way not to fall victim to this fraud is to sell or exit your position quickly. Do not aim for high profits. Another thing that you can do is to exit a part of your investment, and then leave another part of it to continue to ride and take advantage of the scheme. Still, to be in the position of profit, you should keep in mind to exit your position *before* the cryptocurrency gets dumped.

CHAPTER 7

PROFESSIONAL TRADING PRACTICES

✓ Research and analysis

Research and analysis should be the center of your activities as a cryptocurrency investor/trader. You cannot expect to make continuous profits in the market unless you are willing and actually do actual research and analysis. Needless to say, this is something that you should do on a regular basis. After all, this is the only way that you can gain an understanding of the cryptocurrency market. Without the right understanding, then you would not be able to come up with the right decisions. Therefore, continue to study the market. Make sure to follow the latest news, join related groups and forums, and learn as much as you can. Knowledge is the key to success. Do not forget that the cryptocurrency market does not work randomly. If you can get the right information and be able to analyze it properly, then you can identify profitable investments that you can make. Without continuous research and analysis, then it would also be impossible to make continuous profits in the cryptocurrency market.

It is also important that you do sufficient research. It is true that many investors and traders do their research before making an investment; however, a very common mistake is to do so little research. Just because you have spent three hours on your computer trying to understand the market does not mean that you are already in the position to make the best and profitable investment. You should know that true professional and successful traders spend hours every day studying and analyzing the market, and yet they are still very careful each time they make a trade or investment. Never enter any position or make any investment without doing enough research and analysis.

✓ Only invest the money that you can afford to lose

This is a common advice that is given to casino gamblers. The truth is that there is no amount of preparation and research that can guarantee that a particular investment will end up in your favor. The cryptocurrency market is highly volatile, and there are simply so many things that can happen in the course of an investment. Therefore, you should never use the money that you need to pay for your electric bill and other obligations. This is also a good way not to be too pressured. When you use the money that you need for your obligations, you will not be able to think clearly. Therefore, only invest the money that you can afford to lose. This way you will not be pressured even if you encounter a losing investment. This will allow you to think more clearly and effectively.

✓ Self-discipline

Self-discipline is extremely important to your success. Unfortunately, many investors and traders learn about it the hard way. Normally, they only realize the importance of self-discipline after losing an investment. This is another reason why experts advise that you should only start out small when you are a beginner. This way you can learn about self-discipline and make mistakes without risking too much. Self-discipline is also the best way to combat greed. As you may already know, greed is a serious enemy. It has caused many investors to lose their profits and investments. A good way to exercise discipline is to have a plan. You should set a short-term plan and a long-term plan even before you invest in anything. It is a good practice to already decide on how much profit that you reasonably expect to make from a particular investment. For example, if you think that it is only reasonable to make 20% profit, then you should close your position as soon as you reach your 20% profit objective. It is advised that you should remain as conservative as possible. Stick to your strategy and the plan that you have set. Of course, the only exception to not sticking to your plan is if there are good reasons to believe based on facts that taking another course of action would be the better option.

✓ Cryptocurrency trading journal

Although having a trading journal is not required, there

are many experts who strongly recommend it. The reason is that a trading journal will allow you to see yourself from a new perspective that is free from any form of bias and/or prejudice. It will also allow you to learn things that you might not be able to realize unless with the use of a journal. Do not worry; keeping a journal is not easy, and you do not have to be a good writer just to maintain a trading journal. However, there are two things that you need to do: You need to be completely honest, and you need to update your journal regularly.

Since it is your trading journal, you can write anything and everything that you want as long as it is related to your life as cryptocurrency investor. Ideally, your journal should include your reasons why you want to invest in cryptocurrencies, the strategies that you use, your past and current trading positions or investments, the mistakes and lessons that you have learned, and others. Be open and honest at the same time.

In the first few weeks, you may not find your trading journal to be very valuable; however, if you persist for a few more weeks, you will soon realize just how valuable and helpful it is once you read your journal. You will see just how much you grow and mature as a cryptocurrency investor/trader.

✓ Professional approach

Although there is nothing wrong with participating in the market as a mere hobby or just for fun, you also should not expect to make so much profit with it if you only take it as a mere hobby. Approaching it just as a hobby usually signifies lack of dedication and commitment. You should understand that true professional and successful cryptocurrency investors and traders take this work seriously. They spend hours in research just to better understand a single cryptocurrency. This amount and level of hard work and dedication also explain how come they continue to make profits while the others are losing their investments. If you are serious about making profits, then it is strongly advised that you should take this activity seriously as you would any other business or profession. Be professional and act professionally.

✓ Practice

You cannot be a successful and experience cryptocurrency investor simply by reading books on how to invest in the cryptocurrency market. Being a successful investor or trader takes actual practice. You need to practice how to apply the strategies effectively and properly. You should also develop your own strategy. You should understand that the strategies in this book only serve to give you an idea of how professional traders deal with the market, but these strategies should not limit your creativity. Feel free to explore and develop your own strategy. When working on a strategy, it is good to take advantage of the demo account that is provided by your broker, if any. If there is no demo account that you can use, simply start out using very small investments to test your strategy. Other than reading about the cryptocurrency market, you should engage in the actual practice. Becoming a professional and successful trader is like learning a new skill. It takes actual practice. Hence, continue to practice the different strategies, feel free to modify them, and even with an entirely new and unique strategy of your own.

✓ Take a break

It is easy to get absorbed into the activities of being a cryptocurrency investor. It is not uncommon to find people who do not notice the time as they analyze the market and the different cryptocurrencies that they can invest in. Although it is good to work hard, you should also understand that taking a break is also important. By allowing yourself to take a break, you will be able to clear your mind and relax your body. This will allow you to be able to think more clearly and effectively. As a result, you will be able to come up with better decisions. When you take a break, that is the time for you not to think about the cryptocurrency market or anything that has any relation to it. Enjoy your time of fun and relaxation. Do not worry; after taking a break, you are expected to work even harder. It is noteworthy that you should only give yourself a chance to take a break only if you have rendered some hard work; otherwise, there is no reason for you to take a break. Keep in mind that taking a break is not an excuse for being lazy. You still need to work hard and to work continuously.

✓ Patience

As they say, patience is a virtue. Indeed, the same is true when you deal with the cryptocurrency market. You need to learn to be patient and observe proper timing. A common mistake is to keep on investing and trading even when the market is down. Of course, there is still an opportunity to make a profit, but the chances are low. Sometimes the best way to deal with the market is to be inactive. Simply be patient and observe the market. Soon enough, a better opportunity will arise, and be sure that you will be ready to take advantage of it. Professional and successful investors know that just because they have spent hours studying the market does not always mean that they should open a position or make any investment. Remember the rule that you should only make an investment if there are good reasons to believe based on facts that such investment is most likely end up to be profitable. If the market is down, then exercise patience. Patience and hard work can be highly rewarding in the long run.

✓ Enjoy

Although being a cryptocurrency investor can be sad in the sense that you immerse yourself in a market that does not care about you, there are perks that you can enjoy. Enjoy the fact that you are your own boss, you have complete control over your schedule, and that you can earn a very high amount of profit. You can also function more effectively if you are enjoying what you are doing. Hence, enjoy all the readings and research that you are doing as a trader. If you are not interested in the cryptocurrency market, you might not be able to make a profit from it. You must develop some kind of passion in what you are doing. Enjoy the work and the life of a cryptocurrency investor/trader. This is a fun and adventurous life that can be rewarding in the long run. Although there is no assurance if any investment will turn out profitably or not, you can always decide to fun and enjoy what you are doing.

CONCLUSION

Thanks for making it through to the end of this book. We hope it was informative and able to provide you with all of the tools you need to achieve your goals whatever they may be.

The next step is to apply everything that you have learned and start raking in serious profits. So, what are you waiting for? It is time for you to create a cryptocurrency wallet, open an account with a reliable broker, and start turning your knowledge into profits.

The cryptocurrency market remains to be a highly lucrative market for those who understand how it works. With the right knowledge as provided and revealed in this book and continuous hard work, you can make your way to success and financial freedom.

Finally, if you found this book useful in anyway, a review on Amazon is always appreciated!

If you want you can subscribe to our newsletter: http://bit.ly/2EZWzlJ